Crafting
Your
LEADERSHIP
LEGACY

A Guided Journal

EMBRACE | **DESIGN** | **CREATE**
Your Vision | Your Plan | Your Legacy

Crafting
Your
LEADERSHIP
LEGACY

A Guided Journal

Heather Gillette ✤ Barbara Martin

co-founders of Lead-ology Consulting LLC

[lead]-ology
PUBLISHING

Published by Lead-ology Publishing

[lead]-ology
PUBLISHING

Printed in the United States of America.
First edition 2025.

Cover and layout design by G Sharp Design, LLC.
www.gsharpmajor.com

ISBN 979-8-9929558-0-4 (paperback)

This book would not be possible without a series of events in our leadership journey that brought us together with retired Navy captain and former Washington State PTA Executive Director Kathryn M. Hobbs.

We met Kathryn when she was hired by Washington State PTA as we began our term as state president and vice president. She was adamant about the importance of leaving a legacy that would not only sustain our own leadership journey but also the association for years to come. She has always led by encouraging innovative thought and applauding courage for stepping outside of our comfort zones. Working with Kathryn was a masterclass in business.

So, Kathryn, this book is dedicated to you. You have our love and respect always.

"A mentor is not someone who walks ahead of us and tells us how they did it. A mentor is someone who walks alongside us to guide us on what we can do."

—Simon Sinek

PREFACE

When it comes to leadership, few stories are as powerful as those that highlight a person's growth and lasting impact. As we explore leadership principles and practices, it's important to look both inward and outward.

In this journal, you'll find more than just space for your thoughts. It's a place to capture the story of your personal growth, professional development, and the mark you leave on those around you. Each entry is a chance to reflect on the challenges you've faced, the lessons you've learned, and the values that guide you.

As you start this journey, we hope this journal helps you lead with courage, empathy, and integrity, creating a legacy that inspires future leaders. Embrace your vision, design your plan, and create your legacy, letting your leadership shine brightly for those who follow.

TABLE OF CONTENTS

Design Your Plan

Create Your Legacy

INTRODUCTION

Leadership is one of the most rewarding yet challenging journeys a person can undertake. It requires vision, resilience, and an unwavering commitment to growth—not just for yourself but for the people and organizations you serve. While leadership is often seen as action-oriented and forward-facing, the greatest leaders know that true impact starts with introspection. *Crafting Your Leadership Legacy: A Guided Journal* was created as a tool to help you cultivate that reflective practice, empowering you to lead with purpose and leave a meaningful legacy.

At Lead-ology Consulting, we understand the complexities of leadership because we've been there. With over forty years of combined nonprofit leadership experience and multiple awards for excellence, we've worked alongside countless leaders to help them grow, adapt, and create meaningful change. Through our classes, webinars, and position-specific trainings, we've provided leaders with practical tools and actionable strategies to lead effectively. *Crafting Your Leadership Legacy* is a natural extension of that mission—a resource designed to bring our expertise directly to you in a format that fosters reflection, growth, and intentional leadership.

This journal is more than just a tool; it's a space for you to pause, reflect, and chart your unique path. Whether you're just stepping into a leadership role, navigating the challenges of mid-career decisions, or reflecting on decades of experience, this journal will guide you to explore the values, goals, and lessons that define your leadership. By intentionally documenting your journey, you'll gain clarity on your purpose, deepen your self-awareness, and make deliberate choices that align with the legacy you want to leave behind.

Inside, you'll find thoughtfully crafted prompts and exercises designed to help you:

- reflect on your personal values, strengths, and areas for growth
- set meaningful goals and track your progress over time
- capture important lessons from successes, failures, and pivotal moments, and
- articulate the legacy you want to create and the impact you want to leave on those you lead

As you work through this journal, remember that leadership is not about perfection. It's about progress, intention, and authenticity. This is your opportunity to document your story, learn from your experiences, and design a legacy that reflects your true self.

Take this moment to embrace your leadership journey, one reflection at a time. Your legacy starts here.

Welcome to *Crafting Your Leadership Legacy*—a space for transformation, growth, and purpose-driven leadership, brought to you by Lead-ology Consulting.

FROM VISION TO REALITY: SETTING THE STAGE FOR YOUR LEADERSHIP LEGACY

Introducing *Crafting Your Leadership Legacy*, the perfect companion for leaders at every stage of their journey. Whether you're a seasoned executive or just starting to stretch your leadership wings, this journal is here to help you explore your path to self-discovery and meaningful leadership.

In today's fast-paced world, the challenges leaders face are constantly changing, and that's where *Crafting Your Leadership Legacy* comes in. Think of it as your trusted guide, helping you navigate the ups and downs of leadership with clarity and purpose. Within its pages, you'll embark on a transformative journey of introspection, goal setting, and skill development.

By documenting your values, aspirations, and daily reflections, you'll develop the habits of self-awareness and resilience— essential for effective leadership. Moreover, this journal isn't just about personal growth; it's about crafting a legacy that lasts. Through exercises such as legacy crafting, impact assessment, and succession planning, you'll ensure that your leadership journey leaves a meaningful imprint on those you lead and the organizations you serve.

In a world that craves authentic and visionary leaders, *Crafting Your Leadership Legacy* is not just a tool—*it's a legacy in the making!*

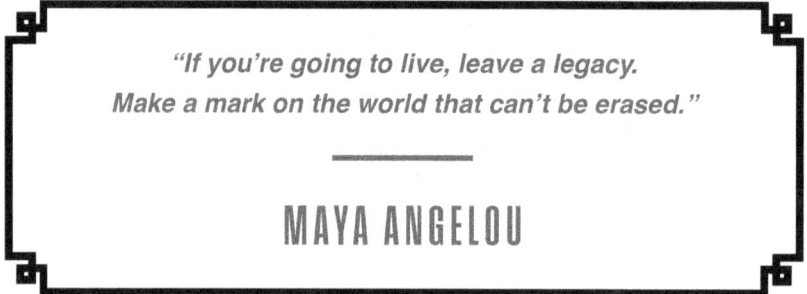

"If you're going to live, leave a legacy. Make a mark on the world that can't be erased."

MAYA ANGELOU

What Is Leadership?

Crafting Your Leadership Legacy goes beyond capturing thoughts and reflections; it represents the enduring principles of leadership. At its core, leadership is not merely a position or title but a profound commitment to inspire, empower, and effect positive change. It embodies the art of influence, the science of strategy, and the essence of service. Leadership is about forging a path forward, not just for oneself but for others, leaving behind a legacy that goes far beyond individual accomplishments.

When talking about leadership, one concept that really stands out is legacy. It's all about the lasting impact that leaders have on people, organizations, and communities—not just in the moment but for years to come. A leader's legacy reflects their values, vision, and ability to inspire others to grow and improve together. To create a meaningful legacy, leaders need to build trust, empower their team, and create an environment where everyone can learn and innovate. By focusing on leaving a lasting legacy, leaders not only ensure that their contributions will endure but also inspire future generations to lead with excellence and purpose. It's not just something to aspire to—it's a responsibility to make the world a better place through our leadership.

This journal starts with the big question: what is leadership, really? It's something that can mean so many different things to different people, and it is important to make space for exploring those different perspectives. Through deep thinking and personal reflection, it is possible to unpack all the complexities of leadership and get to the heart of what it really means.

And as you dive into that question, think beyond just the present moment. What kind of legacy do you want to leave as a leader? How does your vision for the future come into play? By looking at personal experiences and finding meaning in them, we hope that each entry in this journal will be a testament to the values, hopes, and dreams of each contributor. It's not just a chance to reflect on your own leadership but to inspire others to lead with vision and purpose and, ultimately, to leave a lasting impact on the world.

How to Use This Journal

This journal was created to help you grow as a leader and to cultivate intentionality in your leadership practice. How? By using the thoughtful writing prompts included in each section.

These prompts were designed to help you explore different aspects of leadership, like your values, experiences, challenges, and aspirations. By engaging with them regularly, you can learn more about yourself, become more self-aware, and get insights into your strengths and areas for development. Plus, by regularly putting pen to paper, you'll start to articulate your thoughts, feelings, and intentions more clearly (which is always a good thing).

Keep in mind that there are no "right" or "wrong" answers to these prompts—they are meant to provide an opportunity for you to reflect on your experiences as a leader and think about how you might feel or react in different situations. You might interpret them in multiple ways based on what's going on in your life at the moment. Whether you take each section separately or build your answers across sections is entirely up to you.

One way to use this journal is to work through it on your own, taking time to reflect and journal in a quiet, comfortable space. Or you might want to use it as a guided exercise with other leaders (like your volunteer team or employees). The choice is yours!

STEPS FOR COMPLETION

1. Find a quiet space where you can focus without distractions, and set aside time to work on your journal entries. Make it a regular habit to work on entries.

2. Begin by reflecting on past experiences. Consider both successful and challenging instances, and think about what you learned from each situation.

3. Write your responses to the selected prompts in your journal. Be honest and introspective, and don't be afraid to explore your thoughts and feelings deeply.

4. After completing each entry, take time to reflect on and analyze your responses. Identify areas of strength and areas for improvement in your skills. Develop strategies and action plans to enhance your strengths and address weaknesses.

5. Regularly review your journal entries to track your progress over time. Celebrate achievements and milestones, and adjust your strategies as needed to continue growing as a communicator and leader.

Ready to get started?

Embrace Your Vision

Every leadership journey begins with a clear and inspired vision. It is the foundation on which all meaningful action and lasting impact are built. Without a vision to guide you, leadership can feel like a series of disconnected tasks, rather than a purposeful path toward something greater. That's why this first chapter, "Embrace Your Vision," focuses on helping you uncover and solidify the values, experiences, and inspirations that define your leadership.

"Leadership is the capacity
to influence others through
inspiration motivated
by passion, generated
by vision, produced by
a conviction, ignited
by a purpose."

MYLES MUNROE

UNIT 1

Empowering Words: Inspirational Quotes and Transformative Stories

This unit highlights the power of uplifting words that resonate with your own values and experiences, drawing on the timeless words of inspirational leaders and personal stories. As leaders strive to make a lasting impact, they often find comfort, guidance, and inspiration in the words of those who came before them. Through powerful quotes, meaningful anecdotes, and lessons from overcoming challenges, this unit highlights the power of storytelling in shaping leadership legacies. By sharing experiences and collective wisdom, leaders can create connections, spark passion, and build a legacy that resonates for years to come.

This unit includes three sections of prompts:

- **Quotes from Inspirational Leaders**
- **Personal Stories of Resilience**
- **Lessons Learned from Adversity**

Quotes from Inspirational Leaders

Leadership is often shaped by the wisdom of those who came before us. The words of great leaders can serve as a source of guidance, offering fresh perspectives, renewed motivation, and clarity when we need it most. In this section, we'll explore how these powerful insights can illuminate your own leadership journey.

Start by immersing yourself in the words that speak to you. Whether they resonate because of their timeless truth, a shared experience, or their ability to inspire action, quotes often hold lessons waiting to be unpacked. These lessons can deepen your understanding of what it means to lead with purpose and conviction.

As you reflect, think about the ways these words intersect with your personal and professional experiences. Consider how they align with your values, challenge your assumptions, or help you navigate the complexities of leadership. Each quote is an invitation to not only contemplate its meaning but also integrate its wisdom into how you show up as a leader.

Draw strength from others' words.

Finally, remember that leadership is not just about individual growth—it's about guiding and inspiring others. Some quotes can offer clarity and direction for specific challenges or opportunities you face within your team or organization. Engaging with these insights is an opportunity to broaden your perspective and refine your approach as you work to leave a meaningful legacy.

Quotes from Inspirational Leaders—Journal Prompts

1. **Resonating Quotes:** Identify three quotes that stir something within you. Why did these particular words resonate?

   _____

   _____

   _____

   _____

2. **Growth Quote:** Choose a quote that has profoundly influenced your leadership journey. Reflect on the attributes or messages within it that shape your leadership style. How do these align with the leader you aspire to be?

   _____

   _____

   _____

   _____

3. **Challenge or Opportunity Quote:** Select a quote that speaks directly to a current challenge or moment of opportunity for your team or organization. Discuss the insights or teachings this quote offers and how it could inform your approach at this time.

   _____

   _____

   _____

   _____

MORE TO SAY? No problem! Use the provided lined pages at the end of each unit to capture your thoughts!

Personal Stories of Resilience

In this section, the focus is on the powerful concept of resilience. Start with a meaningful quote or a story of success that reflects your experiences with challenges, using it to highlight your own struggles and successes. By taking these steps, you will begin to uncover the essence of resilience and the lessons that have strengthened your leadership and response to adversity.

Consider the wisdom gained from these moments—the strategies that helped you overcome obstacles and the insights that now shape your leadership approach. Think about how these lessons extend beyond your personal experience and can help others facing their own difficulties.

Use the chosen quote or story not just as a reminder of past resilience but as a way to connect with other leaders. It's a testament to the shared journey of overcoming challenges and a guide to turning adversity into growth.

Celebrate your journey's tests and triumphs.

Finally, emphasize the power of perseverance. Leadership that remains strong during tough times not only builds personal resolve but also inspires others to rise above their challenges, creating a legacy of strength and perseverance.

Personal Stories of Resilience–Journal Prompts

1. **Resilience:** Describe a defining moment where your resilience shone through, in either your personal journey or leadership role, and how it shaped the outcome.

   _____

   _____

   _____

   _____

   _____

2. **Qualities of Resilience:** Identify and discuss the attributes that embody resilience. How do these qualities influence and enhance your leadership approach?

   _____

   _____

   _____

   _____

   _____

3. **Perseverance:** Relay a personal account of facing a significant challenge. Elaborate on the resilience you harnessed to prevail and the particular traits that supported your perseverance.

   _____

   _____

   _____

   _____

   _____

Lessons Learned from Adversity

Adversity comes in various forms, such as facing a setback in one's career. However, one of the most profound lessons we learn from adversity is how to conduct ourselves amidst it. How we react to adversity can define our character and determine our success in overcoming the challenges that lay ahead of us. It is important to remain calm, composed, and focused during difficult times. The decisions we make during trying times will ultimately shape our future, and a hasty or negative approach may lead to regret.

Growth is another essential lesson learned from adversity. Experiencing hardship allows us to see things from a different perspective, to reevaluate our priorities, and to understand the importance of resilience. It is often through our struggles that

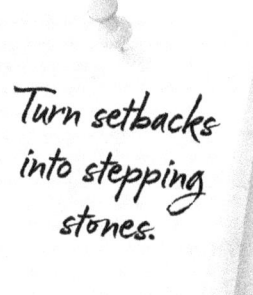

Turn setbacks into stepping stones.

we uncover our true strengths, and we learn to harness them to overcome adversity. Adversity can also help us to develop empathy and appreciation for the struggles of others. It allows us to connect with others who have faced similar challenges and to develop a sense of community, which can be a powerful tool in overcoming adversity.

Ultimately, by persevering through adversity, we can gain a deeper understanding of ourselves and develop the skills we need to navigate life's inevitable challenges with grace and determination.

Lessons Learned from Adversity–Journal Prompts

1. **Lessons in Adversity:** Identify three significant lessons adversity has imparted upon you that have enriched and fortified your leadership.

   _____

   _____

   _____

   _____

   _____

2. **Conduct amid Adversity:** Explore how a leader's conduct amid adversity can serve as a rallying point, inspiring others to persist and prevail.

   _____

   _____

   _____

   _____

   _____

3. **Growth through Adversity:** Recount an instance of significant challenge you've encountered and describe the insights learned, detailing how these have informed your leadership journey.

   _____

   _____

   _____

   _____

   _____

Additional Notes Pages

_____

_____

_____

_____

_____

_____

_____

_____

_____

_____

_____

_____

_____

_____

_____

_____

_____

_____

_____

_____

_____

_____

_____

_____

_____

_____

Additional Notes Pages

"Reflection is one of the most underused yet powerful tools for success."

RICHARD CARLSON

UNIT 2

Journey Within: Unlocking Insights through Reflective Journaling

As you continue your journey, this unit of your journal is designed to help you establish and maintain a regular practice of reflection and journaling. This section serves as a space for introspection, insight, and personal growth, helping you understand yourself better and make positive changes in your life. By consistently engaging in reflection and journaling, you'll gain clarity, perspective, and wisdom, uncovering invaluable insights that highlight your path forward as a leader. Embrace vulnerability, curiosity, and authenticity as you proceed through the complexities of leadership and cultivate a legacy of purpose, impact, and meaningful contribution.

Whether this journal is the spark you need to help you create an ongoing habit of journaling or if you already are committed to journaling, these sections will help shape the effectiveness of your journaling outcomes.

This unit includes three sections of prompts:

- **Daily Reflections**
- **Weekly Insights**
- **Monthly Reviews**

Daily Reflections

The "Daily Reflections" section is meant to help spark introspection and personal growth. Make time each day for this reflection; find a quiet moment to immerse yourself in your thoughts, align with your inner voice, and learn from life's lessons. Use this space to gain clarity with guiding questions that dig into your leadership philosophy.

Let authenticity guide you, and see vulnerability as a strength. Consider your entire leadership journey—the wins that uplift you, the challenges that test you, and the steady progress in between.

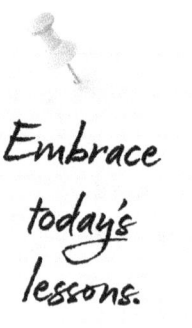

Embrace today's lessons.

Commit to this practice of self-examination beyond this journal, knowing that each entry helps you understand yourself better as a leader. Regularly reviewing your thoughts will reveal patterns, show your growth, and provide new perspectives on your leadership journey.

Approach your "Daily Reflections" with a desire to uncover truth, a readiness to change, and a commitment to gain insights that shape a leadership style that is both genuine and effective. This is the path to creating a legacy of meaningful action and authentic leadership.

Daily Reflections—Journal Prompts

1. **Value of Daily Reflection to Leadership:** Recall a recent event that drove your commitment to daily introspection and how it has impacted various facets of your life, personally and professionally.

   _____

   _____

   _____

   _____

   _____

2. **Guiding Questions:** How have these inquiries facilitated deeper understanding, helped in recognizing recurrent themes, and supported you in crafting your intentions for subsequent days?

   _____

   _____

   _____

   _____

   _____

3. **Obstacles to Daily Reflection:** Explore strategies you've used to overcome these challenges and maintain your commitment to continuous personal development.

   _____

   _____

   _____

   _____

   _____

Weekly Insights

The "Weekly Insights" section is an important part of your journal where you bring together your daily reflections into broader patterns of wisdom and purpose. Each week, take time to reflect—an important time to knit together the experiences of the past days. This is your chance to think about your victories, struggles, lessons learned, and the quiet moments of growth.

Connect the detailed notes from your daily entries to the bigger picture of your leadership journey. Look for recurring themes and patterns, finding lessons that match your core values and goals. Each weekly entry should be a clear step in your progress, marking your achievements and pointing the way to future improvement.

When you write your weekly insights, do so with energy and clarity. Use these reflections to not only tell your story but also to guide your actions and decisions as a leader. Embrace the challenge of finding deep understanding in your reflections and let them help shape and refine your leadership practice.

Weave weekly wisdom.

With each weekly entry, you reaffirm your commitment to personal growth. Through thoughtful reflection, curiosity, and a strong drive for improvement, you uncover valuable insights that lead you toward purposeful and effective leadership.

Weekly Insights—Journal Prompts

1. **Benefits for Deeper Insight:** Recount a particularly impactful week—be it through obstacles faced, victories secured, or a-ha moments—and distill the big takeaways or lessons that emerged, explaining how they molded your outlook and objectives.

   _____

   _____

   _____

   _____

   _____

2. **Absorb, Learn, and Uphold Priorities:** Describe how this ritual has helped you organize the week's experiences into actionable wisdom.

   _____

   _____

   _____

   _____

   _____

3. **Identify Changes:** Articulate how these refinements have fostered your development and enhanced your approach to leadership.

   _____

   _____

   _____

   _____

   _____

Monthly Reviews

The "Monthly Reviews" section is the third part of your reflective journaling, tying together the perspectives of your daily and weekly journaling. It offers a chance to step back and look at your leadership journey from a higher perspective. As each month ends, set aside time to reflect on your daily and weekly experiences and put them together into a complete story. Look over the past month, noting your achievements, challenges, and lessons learned along the way.

Dive deep into this reflection, celebrating your successes and thoughtfully examining the obstacles you've faced. Use this monthly practice to see how your daily decisions align with your larger leadership goals and core values. Treat your journal as a trusted friend, documenting your journey with honesty and insight and creating a detailed picture of your growing leadership style.

Harvest monthly milestones.

When writing your monthly reflections, strive for balance and understanding. Recognize that every step—whether forward or backward—contributes to your growth. Celebrate your successes with gratitude, learn from every experience, and set clear goals for the future that align with your vision. The "Monthly Reviews" are not just summaries but important steps toward building a leadership legacy defined by ongoing learning, thoughtful actions, and a strong commitment to personal growth.

Monthly Reviews–Journal Prompts

1. **Stay on Track:** Elaborate on how engaging in monthly reviews serves as a compass to keep your leadership journey on track, monitors progress, and ensures fidelity to your long-term aspirations.

   _____

   _____

   _____

   _____

2. **Examine Obstacles:** Identify the probing questions that steer your monthly reviews. How do questions like "What were my triumphs this month?" or "Where can I improve?" facilitate a comprehensive evaluation of your recent experiences and help in building the roadmap for the upcoming month?

   _____

   _____

   _____

   _____

3. **Balance and Understanding:** Examine any recurring themes or developments that have become apparent through your monthly reviews. How do these patterns shed light on your leadership evolution and guide your plans for ongoing refinement and development?

   _____

   _____

   _____

   _____

Additional Notes Pages

_____

_____

_____

_____

_____

_____

_____

_____

_____

_____

_____

_____

_____

_____

_____

_____

_____

_____

_____

_____

_____

_____

_____

_____

Additional Notes Pages

"The best way to succeed is to have a specific intent, a clear vision, a plan of action, and the ability to maintain clarity."

STEVE MARABOLI

UNIT 3

Envisioning Success: Crafting Vision Boards and Mastering Visualization

People have dominant traits that enhance learning. For example, this journal is a physical learning tool, as the actions of writing reinforce the learning. This unit is for the visual learners and is all about using visual tools to help plan and turn your leadership dreams into reality. As a leader, it's important to clearly show your aspirations and guide your team toward shared success. Creating vision boards, visualizing your future self, and making detailed action plans can be meaningful steps in this process.

Start by exploring the power of vision boards. These are visual representations of your goals and dreams, helping you to see and stay focused on what you want to achieve. Next, practice visualizing your future self. Imagine the leader you want to become and the impact you want to have. This helps you stay motivated and aligned with your long-term goals.

Finally, create strategic action plans. Break down your big dreams into smaller, actionable steps. This makes your goals more manageable and helps you track your progress. By combining these tools, you can clearly articulate your vision, stay focused on your goals, and make a lasting impact on your leadership journey.

This unit includes three sections of prompts:

- **Visual Representation of Goals**
- **Future Self Visualization**
- **Action Plans**

Visual Representation of Goals

"Visual Representation of Goals" is all about bringing your ambitions to life through visualization. This technique encourages you to choose a goal that truly excites you and create a clear vision of achieving it. You can do this by making a vision board filled with inspiring images and affirmations or by vividly imagining the steps to your success in your mind. Visualization can be a strong and life-changing habit.

As you work through this section, think about how visualization has helped you in the past. What practices have been most effective in moving you toward your goals? Think about your experiences with creating vision boards and your daily visualization habits that have kept you on track.

Picture your path clearly.

Also, consider how visualization can impact your leadership. How can it help you overcome limitations and foster a mindset geared toward success? Reflect on how you can incorporate this strategy into your leadership development, helping both yourself and your team achieve shared goals.

Visual Representation of Goals–Journal Prompts

1. **Visualization as a Tool:** Recount an instance when visualization became an important tool in surmounting challenges on your path to a goal. Detail how envisioning the outcome helped dispel doubts and moved you toward success.

   _____

   _____

   _____

   _____

2. **Use of Visual Mediums:** Identify a current ambition, and bring it to life through a creative visual medium like a vision board, sketch, or mind map. Discuss the impact this visualization process had on your motivation and strategy to realize this goal.

   _____

   _____

   _____

   _____

3. **Developing an Action Plan:** Map out the journey to one of your goals with clarity and precision. Craft a step-by-step action plan, complete with a realistic timeline, visualizing each milestone and envisioning the successful achievement of your goal.

   _____

   _____

   _____

   _____

MINDSET

LEGACY

PROFESSIONAL

VISION BOARD
(SAMPLE)

RELATIONSHIPS

HOME

MIND MAPPING (SAMPLE)

MAIN IDEA OR TOPIC

IDEA

IDEA

IDEA

RELATED IDEA

RELATED IDEA

RELATED IDEA

SUB IDEA

SUB IDEA

SUB IDEA

RELATED IDEA

RELATED IDEA

RELATED IDEA

SUB IDEA

SUB IDEA

SUB IDEA

Future-Self Visualization

"Future-Self Visualization" is an empowering technique to help you chart the course for the person you want to become. Start by clearly imagining your future—identify the qualities, achievements, and impact you aim to realize. This is about defining your aspirations and mapping out your potential.

Visualize the person you are working toward—your character, your successes, and the mark you want to make on the world. Solidifying this vision boosts your motivation, strengthens your resolve, and helps you navigate potential obstacles.

Create a visual representation of your future self through a vision board or another creative method. This serves as a constant reminder of your direction and goals, linking today's actions with tomorrow's results and providing stability during uncertain times.

Envision, then become.

While visualization sets the stage, it's the combination of these vivid images with commitment and action-able steps that brings your future into reality. Use this section as a space for dreaming and planning but also for taking concrete actions—each a vital part of turning your vision into the life you desire and the leader you want to become.

Future-Self Visualization–Journal Prompts

1. **Five-Year Vision:** Visualize where you stand five years from now, having realized a pivotal personal or professional ambition. Paint a clear picture of your achievements, and express the emotions accompanying this success.

   _____

   _____

   _____

   _____

2. **Areas for Development:** Select an area in your life—be it in your relationships, career, or personal well-being—where you aspire to see transformative development. Illustrate what triumph looks like and how it shapes the person you aim to become.

   _____

   _____

   _____

   _____

3. **Characteristics of Successful Leaders:** Consider a leader who embodies the essence of success to you. Identify the characteristics or accomplishments you admire and how they inform the leadership qualities you strive to cultivate within yourself.

   _____

   _____

   _____

   _____

Action Plans

Action plans bridge the gap between your dreams and the realities you want to achieve. This section emphasizes turning vivid visualizations into tangible steps. While visualizing your goals is powerful, it's your commitment to taking action that makes those dreams come true.

Start by breaking down your big aspirations into specific, attainable actions. Divide your grand ambitions into smaller tasks organized by priority and sequence. The key to an actionable plan is clarity—outlining each step with clear timelines and measurable milestones.

Blueprint your success journey.

Leaders have many tools at their disposal to chart their path—whether it's creating a vision board, using mind maps, or drawing sketches. Choose the method that resonates with your style and complements your strategic thinking. Your action plan should be a clear, practical roadmap, one that you revisit and refine regularly to stay on course in your leadership journey.

Action Plans–Journal Prompts

1. **Look Behind to Move Ahead:** Revisit a time when you faced difficulties in realizing an ambition. Looking back, what steps could have helped build a stronger action plan to reach that goal?

   _____

   _____

   _____

   _____

2. **Steps for Current Challenge:** Identify a challenge you're currently facing. Detail the actionable steps you can take to overcome this obstacle, and specify the immediate actions you will initiate to put your plan into motion.

   _____

   _____

   _____

   _____

3. **Metrics to Assess Success:** Describe the metrics you will use to track the success of your action plan. How will you remain flexible and ready to recalibrate your strategy to navigate unforeseen changes?

   _____

   _____

   _____

   _____

Action Plan Template

GOAL:						
Action Step	Responsible	Start Date	Milestones	Due Date	Resources	Desired Outcomes

Additional Notes Pages

_____

_____

_____

_____

_____

_____

_____

_____

_____

_____

_____

Additional Notes Pages

"Knowing what's right
doesn't mean much unless
you do what's right."

THEODORE ROOSEVELT

UNIT 4

Ethics at the Core: Navigating Ethical Dilemmas and Promoting Civility

---

Within the framework of leadership legacy, this unit emphasizes the fundamental principles that form the backbone of effective leadership. True leadership isn't just about hitting targets or winning awards; it's about creating an environment built on respect, integrity, and trust. This unit explores the essential aspects of promoting respectful dialogue, making ethical decisions, and fostering trust and accountability.

By adhering to these principles, leaders can navigate challenges with clarity and a strong moral compass, building a culture where integrity thrives. Great leaders understand that their legacy is defined not only by their achievements but also by the ethical foundation that supports those successes. Through a commitment to ethical behavior and civility, leaders can create a lasting legacy that positively influences and inspires others.

This unit includes three sections of prompts:

- Promoting Respectful Dialogue
- Ethical Decision-Making
- Building Trust and Accountability

Promoting Respectful Dialogue

Navigating leadership complexities requires fostering an environment of mutual respect and open communication. Start by considering and understanding the basics of respectful dialogue and effective leadership.

Think about how active listening, empathy, and inclusivity are essential for meaningful conversations. Look into strategies for resolving conflicts peacefully and maintaining respect, such as setting clear ground rules, practicing mindfulness, and using mediation tools. These techniques not only address conflicts but also build a culture of respect and understanding.

Remember that promoting respectful dialogue is an important part of effective leadership. It's important for fostering teamwork, sparking new ideas, and building trust within your team. Reflect on your own experiences, and think about how you can promote a culture of respectful dialogue in your leadership practices, making sure every voice is heard and valued.

Foster open, honest exchanges.

Approach the "Promoting Respectful Dialogue" prompts with empathy, openness, and a commitment to continuous improvement. This will help you lead with integrity and create a positive, collaborative work environment.

Promoting Respectful Dialogue—Journal Prompts

1. **Fostering Civility:** What is your responsibility in fostering an environment of civility? Provide a list of ways to promote respectful dialogue, active listening, and constructive disagreement among team members.

   _____

   _____

   _____

   _____

2. **Empathetic Communication:** Elaborate on how empathetic communication practices can enhance understanding, build trust, and facilitate constructive conversations in diverse organizational settings.

   _____

   _____

   _____

   _____

3. **Culture and Legacy:** Share personal experiences or examples of leaders who have effectively demonstrated empathy in their communication strategies, and explore the long-term impact of cultivating an empathetic leadership style on organizational culture and legacy.

   _____

   _____

   _____

   _____

Ethical Decision-Making

Making ethical choices with integrity is crucial for effective leadership. This section of *Crafting Your Leadership Legacy* invites you to explore the principles and practices of ethical decision-making. Begin by reflecting on the core concepts of "ethical decision-making" and "leadership," setting the stage for a deeper examination of your own ethical experiences.

Think about times when you've faced ethical dilemmas in your leadership roles. What processes did you use to handle these situations? Highlight the importance of upholding ethical principles and maintaining integrity. Look into various frameworks or models that help assess risks, weigh consequences, and make informed ethical decisions.

Next, focus on strategies and tools that support leaders in maintaining ethical standards. Discuss the role of ethical awareness, moral reasoning, and accountability in promoting a culture of ethical leadership. Emphasize the value of seeking diverse perspectives, encouraging open dialogue, and creating an environment where ethics are prioritized.

Choose integrity over convenience.

Finally, consider the broader impact of ethical decision-making on your leadership legacy. Reflect on how consistent ethical choices can shape organizational culture, build trust, and leave a lasting positive impact. Embrace ethical decision-making as a continuous journey of growth and learning, reinforcing your dedication to leading with integrity and purpose.

By approaching the "Ethical Decision-Making" prompts thoughtfully and transparently, you can strengthen your leadership and inspire others to follow your example.

Ethical Decision-Making–Journal Prompts

1. **Prioritizing Ethics:** Reflect on how you prioritize integrity, honesty, and fairness in your leadership approach.

   _____

   _____

   _____

   _____

2. **Uphold Ethical Standards:** Share an ethical dilemma you have faced. What were the steps taken to uphold your ethical standards, even when faced with pressure or temptation?

   _____

   _____

   _____

   _____

3. **Ethical Growth:** Reflect on a time when you faced a difficult decision that involved ethical considerations. Describe the decision-making process you used and how you ultimately reached your decision. In hindsight, what would you have done differently, and what did you learn from the experience?

   _____

   _____

   _____

   _____

Building Trust and Accountability

Recognizing the foundational role of trust and accountability is another important function for effective leadership and organizational success. As you begin this section, start by defining trust and accountability, highlighting their importance in fostering a positive workplace environment.

Reflect on your personal and professional experiences where trust and accountability were either present or lacking. Use these examples to illustrate their impact on team dynamics, morale, and overall performance.

Consider the role of transparent communication, integrity, and shared values in building trust. Explore methods for holding individuals and teams accountable, providing concrete steps and strategies for leaders to implement.

Be consistent & transparent.

Conclude by emphasizing the long-term benefits of prioritizing trust and accountability in leadership practices, underscoring their contribution to a legacy of ethical conduct and civility within the organization.

Building Trust and Accountability—Journal Prompts

1. **Strategies:** What are two strategies for fostering transparency, demonstrating consistency, and holding yourself and others accountable for their actions?

   _____

   _____

   _____

   _____

   _____

2. **Trust and Accountability:** How can leaders define trust and accountability in their leadership styles?

   _____

   _____

   _____

   _____

   _____

3. **Building Trust:** What strategies can leaders use to build trust and accountability in their workplaces?

   _____

   _____

   _____

   _____

   _____

Additional Notes Pages

_____

_____

_____

_____

_____

_____

_____

_____

_____

_____

_____

_____

_____

_____

_____

_____

_____

_____

_____

_____

_____

_____

_____

_____

_____

_____

_____

_____

_____

Additional Notes Pages

Design Your Plan

A vision without a plan is simply a dream. To transform your vision into a reality, you need a roadmap that connects your purpose with meaningful action. This chapter, "Design Your Plan," is where clarity meets strategy, helping you craft intentional steps to align your leadership journey with your goals and values.

"Leadership is about
making others better
as a result of your
presence and making
sure that impact lasts in
your absence."

SHERYL SANDBERG

Measuring Impact: Mapping Leadership Contributions and Influence

Looking back on the impact of one's leadership journey isn't just about reflection—it's an essential part of growth and development. This section serves as a place where leaders can think about the effects of their actions and decisions as they impact individuals, teams, and organizations.

By engaging in thoughtful introspection, leaders can uncover valuable insights into their leadership style, strengths, areas for improvement, and the broader ripple effects of their leadership legacy. Through a balanced exploration of successes, challenges, and lessons they have learned, this section empowers leaders to cultivate a deeper understanding of their impact and pave the path for future growth and effectiveness.

This unit includes three sections of prompts:

- **Assessing Leadership Impact**
- **Successes and Achievements**
- **Challenges and Lessons Learned**

Assessing Leadership Impact

Engaging with the "Assessing Leadership Impact" prompts provides an opportunity to critically examine the breadth and depth of your influence as a leader. Begin this part of your journey by reflecting on the diverse roles you've assumed, the projects you've led, and the teams you've guided. Analyze how your distinctive leadership style has impacted those around you, shaped the outcomes of your initiatives, and influenced the culture of your organization.

Begin by evaluating the effectiveness of your leadership using both quantitative measures, like performance metrics and goal completion rates, and qualitative aspects, such as team morale and engagement. Assess how these indicators align with your core leadership values and objectives, and consider if they fully encapsulate the scope of your impact.

Moreover, confront the times when your leadership has had unintended effects. This involves an honest examination of occasions when your actions did not align with your intentions or led to unexpected challenges. View these instances as invaluable learning opportunities, extracting lessons that will refine your future leadership approaches.

Quantify your influence.

In your considerations, embrace honesty and humility, recognizing both your successes and areas for growth. By approaching the "Assessing Leadership Impact" prompts with curiosity, introspection, and a commitment to continuous learning, you will uncover insights into your leadership practice, setting the stage for meaningful personal and professional development.

Assessing Leadership Impact–Journal Prompts

1. **Examine Your Relationships:** Look back at the relationships you've cultivated and the collaborations you've led throughout your leadership. Describe these dynamics and their significance.

   _____

   _____

   _____

   _____

   _____

2. **Impact of Connections:** Assess how these connections and partnerships have enabled you to effect positive change and achieve your leadership goals. What specific instances demonstrate the power of these relationships?

   _____

   _____

   _____

   _____

   _____

3. **Reflection on Relationship-Building:** Reflect on your approach to building effective relationships. How has this skill amplified your impact and contributed to the success of your initiatives?

   _____

   _____

   _____

   _____

   _____

Successes and Achievements

This section offers leaders a structured opportunity to reflect on and celebrate the important milestones and positive outcomes realized throughout their leadership journey. It is not just a summarization of successes; it's an acknowledgment of the collective effort of teams and the effective strategies that propelled these achievements.

As you begin this reflective journey, take the time to celebrate the victories that have punctuated your experiences. Start by cataloging your most notable accomplishments, which could range from exceeding goals to fostering innovation or steering your organization through turbulent times.

Explore the specifics behind each success: analyze the strategies that were implemented, the decisions that made a difference, and the ways in which your leadership style, communication tactics, and motivational skills played a role in these outcomes. Recognize and appreciate the collaborative efforts of your team and other stakeholders, understanding that true success is a collective achievement.

Celebrate every win.

Document each achievement thoroughly, and reflect on what these successes reveal about your leadership capabilities. Identify consistent elements across different successes, and think about how these strategies can be applied to future challenges. This process should not only reaffirm your strengths but also highlight areas for further refinement.

By engaging with the "Successes and Achievements" prompts thoughtfully, you will enhance your understanding of what makes your leadership effective and how it can be continuously improved, ensuring your future endeavors are even more impactful.

Successes and Achievements–Journal Prompts

1. **Values Alignment:** Reflect on how well your personal values align with those of the organizations or communities you have led. Discuss any challenges and successes you experienced in aligning these values throughout your leadership journey.

    _____

    _____

2. **Cultivating a Values-Driven Culture:** How have you actively fostered a culture that embodies these shared values? Detail the specific strategies you implemented to embed these values deeply within the organization, ensuring they are respected and perpetuated as part of your enduring legacy.

    _____

    _____

3. **Values and Conflict:** Think of a time when a values-driven decision created conflict or tension. What were the strategies you used to navigate this conflict and the outcome of your decision? Discuss the importance of living by your values, even in the face of conflict.

    _____

    _____

Challenges and Lessons Learned

The "Challenges and Lessons Learned" section offers valuable insights into how adversity has shaped your leadership journey. Begin by identifying the major challenges or setbacks you have faced as a leader. These might include navigating organizational changes, overcoming resistance, managing conflicts, or responding to unexpected crises.

After listing these challenges, shift your analysis to the lessons each has imparted. Reflect on your responses to adversity: What strategies proved effective? What insights did you gain about leadership and resilience? Embrace a growth mindset as you dissect these experiences, viewing each not as a setback but as a pivotal learning opportunity.

Document these reflections with an eye toward practical application. Extract actionable insights that will refine your approach to leadership, help you mitigate risks, and prepare you to handle future challenges with greater adeptness. Consider how the experiences have honed your problem-solving skills and decision-making abilities.

Learn, adapt, & overcome.

Furthermore, enhance your understanding by incorporating feedback from mentors, peers, and team members. Their perspectives can provide a broader view of your leadership impact, highlighting strengths and pinpointing areas that need growth.

By engaging with this section's prompts with curiosity, resilience, and a dedication to ongoing self-improvement, you turn adversity into a component of your leadership development, paving the way for enhanced personal and professional growth.

Challenges and Lessons Learned—Journal Prompts

1. **Impact Evaluation:** Evaluate the impact of specific challenges and setbacks on both your personal development and professional growth as a leader. Which experiences had the most significant impact and why?

   _____

   _____

   _____

   _____

2. **Adversity and Resilience:** Reflect on how overcoming adversity has shaped your character and leadership skills. What specific aspects of your resilience have been most transformed through these experiences?

   _____

   _____

   _____

   _____

3. **Insights and Future Navigation:** Consider how these challenging experiences have enriched your understanding of effective leadership. How have they prepared you to navigate future challenges with increased confidence and strategic foresight?

   _____

   _____

   _____

   _____

Additional Notes Pages

_____

_____

_____

_____

_____

_____

_____

_____

_____

_____

_____

_____

_____

_____

_____

_____

_____

_____

_____

_____

_____

_____

_____

_____

_____

_____

_____

Additional Notes Pages

"Leadership and learning
are indispensable to
each other."

JOHN F. KENNEDY

Growing Forward: Skills Development for Emerging Leaders

There are many skills that will enhance the effectiveness of someone's leadership. Skills should be considered as a perpetual journey to get better and not a destination. There is always more to learn, to improve, and to enhance. In this pursuit, honing essential skills is important to leaving a lasting legacy.

Within this unit, we examine the critical domains of communication, decision-making, and emotional intelligence. These pillars not only define a leader's ability to navigate challenges but also shape the culture and success of their teams and organizations. Through deliberate development and application of these skills, leaders can forge a legacy that inspires, empowers, and endures.

This unit includes three sections of prompts:

- **Communication Skills**
- **Decision-Making Skills**
- **Emotional Intelligence**

Communication Skills

Mastering communication skills is fundamental for any leader. Developing a unique voice isn't just about speaking or writing well; it's about making your vision clear and engaging to others. This doesn't require complex vocabulary or lengthy explanations but rather the ability to be concise, clear, and compelling. Effective communication strikes a balance between brevity and sufficiency, providing just enough information to be understood without overwhelming your audience.

This journal section is designed to enhance your communication prowess. Here, you'll engage with prompts crafted to refine your ability to convey your thoughts and ideas effectively. Whether it's verbal presentations or written communications, each prompt is a step toward sharpening your skills. Effective communication is not just about transmitting information—it's about ensuring it's received and understood as intended.

Clarity breeds confidence.

Through consistent practice and your reflections documented in this journal, you'll progress on your journey to becoming not just a stronger leader but a communicator who inspires and motivates. Remember, every entry is an opportunity to improve and become more adept at influencing and leading others through your words.

Communication Skills–Journal Prompts

1. **Resolution through Communication:** Describe a specific instance where effective communication was vital in resolving a conflict or overcoming a significant challenge. What strategies did you employ, and how did they change the outcome?

   _____

   _____

   _____

   _____

2. **Learning from Miscommunication:** Reflect on a particular event where miscommunication led to mis-understanding or conflict. What were the consequences, and what specific steps could you have taken to enhance communication and prevent the issue?

   _____

   _____

   _____

   _____

3. **Admiring Effective Communication:** Identify a leader whose communication style you find effective and inspiring. Discuss the specific qualities or techniques they use that make their communication stand out. How do these strategies influence their leadership effectiveness?

   _____

   _____

   _____

   _____

Decision-Making Skills

Decision-making is a critical skill for an effective leader. This section of your journal invites you to deeply reflect on the decisions you've made throughout your leadership journey. Consider both the decisions that led to success and those that posed challenges. Analyze the factors that influenced these outcomes, whether they were based on intuition, data, consultation, or circumstance.

To engage with this section, consider your current challenges or goals related to decision-making. As you write, detail the context of each decision, your thought process, the emotions involved, and the outcomes. Approach your writing with honesty and introspection, aiming to understand the effectiveness of your decision-making style.

Post-reflection, critically assess your decision-making approach. Identify your strengths—such as quick thinking or thorough risk assessment—and pinpoint areas that need improvement. Develop actionable strategies to enhance your skills in critical thinking, problem-solving, and ethical judgment.

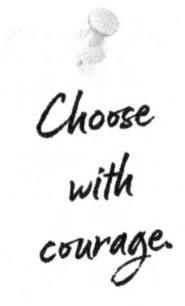

Choose with courage.

Consistently revisit your journal entries to monitor your evolution as a decision-maker. This ongoing practice is designed to help you sharpen your abilities and adapt your strategies, ensuring you grow continuously as a leader equipped to make informed, impactful decisions.

Decision-Making Skills—Journal Prompts

1. **Importance of Decision-Making in Leadership:** Why are decision-making skills critical for effective leadership? Describe the impact of strong decision-making abilities on a leader's success.

   _____

   _____

   _____

   _____

2. **Analyzing a Leadership Decision:** Think back to a particularly challenging decision you made as a leader. What were the main factors that influenced your decision? Describe the process you used to evaluate these factors and how you arrived at your decision.

   _____

   _____

   _____

   _____

3. **Outcomes and Lessons Learned:** Reflecting on the decision discussed above, what were the outcomes? What did this decision reveal about your strengths and weaknesses in decision-making? How have these insights influenced your approach to future leadership challenges?

   _____

   _____

   _____

   _____

Emotional Intelligence

A vital skill set for effective leadership is emotional intelligence. This section of your journal focuses on enhancing your understanding and management of your own emotions, as well as those of others around you. Start by reflecting on instances where you've effectively managed your emotions and situations where you found it challenging.

As you respond to these prompts, be honest and introspective, detailing specific situations where your emotions played a key role in shaping your interactions and outcomes. Consider how emotions influenced your decision-making, communication style, and relationships.

Through your entries, really dig deep into your emotional processes. Analyze how you respond to stress, adapt to change, and recover from setbacks. Identify recurring emotional patterns, recognize triggers, and pinpoint areas where you can improve your emotional control and empathy.

Connect with compassion.

Continuously review your entries to gauge your progress in developing stronger emotional intelligence. This ongoing reflection will help you better understand your emotional landscape, allowing you to make more informed and empathetic decisions. Every entry is not just an exercise but a step toward becoming a more emotionally intelligent leader.

Emotional Intelligence–Journal Prompts

1. **Managing Emotions during Setbacks:** Reflect on a challenging moment in your leadership journey. How did you handle the emotional impact of disappointment, frustration, or self-doubt? Describe the internal and external resources that supported you in managing these emotions.

   _____

   _____

2. **Resilience and Learning from Setbacks:** Building on the previous situation, explore the strategies you implemented to overcome this setback. What did you learn from this experience, and how did it shape your approach to future challenges? Emphasize the role of emotional intelligence in turning obstacles into opportunities for growth.

   _____

   _____

3. **Conflict Resolution Techniques:** Describe a situation where you effectively managed conflict within your team or organization. What strategies did you employ to deescalate tensions and encourage open communication? Detail how these approaches led to solutions that were accepted by all parties involved, and discuss the impact of emotional intelligence in facilitating these outcomes.

   _____

   _____

Additional Notes Pages

Additional Notes Pages

_____

_____

_____

_____

_____

_____

_____

_____

_____

_____

_____

_____

_____

_____

_____

_____

_____

_____

_____

_____

_____

_____

_____

_____

_____

"A goal without a plan is just a wish."

ANTOINE DE SAINT-EXUPERY

Vision into Action: Goal Setting and Achievement Tracking

This unit of your journal is where your journey toward intentional growth and achievement begins. Here, you'll dive into a process of self-discovery, strategic planning, and dream chasing. Think of goal setting as your compass, helping you navigate your leadership journey, while staying organized keeps you on track and ready to adapt as your professional landscape shifts.

Through this section, you'll craft a roadmap for success that reflects your vision, values, and goals. Plus, it's about building accountability and keeping the momentum going as you work toward your leadership ambitions.

This unit includes three sections of prompts:

- **Long-Term Goals**
- **Short-Term Objectives**
- **Progress Tracking**

Long-Term Goals

This section of your journal is your chance to think about and plan the future you want to create. You should consider the big milestones and aspirations that will shape your leadership journey in the years to come. Whether it's reaching career milestones, making a big impact in your industry, or creating positive change in your organization, this is your space to dream big and set a clear path for your future.

Start by thinking about your main leadership goals. Picture where you want to be in the distant future and the legacy you want to leave behind. Write down these long-term goals clearly and confidently, making sure they match your core values and leadership style.

Next, break your long-term goals into smaller, manageable steps. Think about the skills, resources, and experiences you'll need along the way, and anticipate any challenges you might face. Create a clear plan for achieving your long-term goals, including timelines and benchmarks to track your progress.

Envision the endgame.

As you write down your reflections, make sure your long-term goals have a sense of purpose and align with your personal and professional values. Think about how your goals fit into your bigger vision for your leadership legacy and the positive impact you want to have on those you lead.

Approach this "Long-Term Goals" section with intention, strategic thinking, and a commitment to continuous growth. This isn't just about setting goals; it's about creating a legacy that inspires and guides your leadership journey for years to come.

Long-Term Goals—Journal Prompts

1. **Vision and Impact:** Describe the vision you have for your future self, including the impact you hope to make in your profession, community, or field.

   _____

   _____

   _____

   _____

2. **Values and Principles:** Consider the values and principles that guide your long-term goals and the legacy you aspire to leave behind. Describe the steps you are currently taking to work toward these long-term goals, as well as any adjustments or refinements you may need to make to stay aligned with your vision.

   _____

   _____

   _____

   _____

3. **Making Goals Manageable:** Describe the strategies you use to break down big goals into smaller, manageable milestones and the importance of tracking progress and celebrating achievements along the way.

   _____

   _____

   _____

   _____

Short-Term Objectives

This section, "Short-Term Objectives," is designed to help you set and achieve immediate goals that support your long-term vision. It focuses on identifying actionable steps and prioritizing tasks that can be completed soon, driving continuous progress in your leadership journey.

Start by pinpointing the principal priorities and tasks that align with your long-term goals. Break these down into specific, manageable actions that you can complete in the near term. This might include weekly targets, monthly milestones, or quarterly objectives that act as building blocks toward your bigger aspirations.

As you set your short-term objectives, make sure they are clear, specific, and measurable. Clearly state what you aim to achieve, why these objectives matter, and the steps required to accomplish them. Think about any resources, support, or challenges that might impact your progress, and plan strategies to address these factors proactively.

Set achievable milestones.

In documenting your short-term objectives, focus on creating a solid tracking system to monitor your progress. Regularly review and adjust your objectives based on changing circumstances and new insights, ensuring they stay aligned with your overall leadership goals.

By approaching the "Short-Term Objectives" section with determination, precision, and a commitment to action, you can make meaningful, incremental progress that builds toward your long-term success. This section is about making each day count, turning your vision into tangible achievements, and keeping the momentum needed to reach your ultimate leadership aspirations.

Short-Term Objectives—Journal Prompts

1. **Define Your Objectives**: Identify specific short-term objectives that align with your long-term goals. What actions or tasks do you need to accomplish in the next few months to make progress toward your broader aspirations?

   _____

   _____

   _____

   _____

2. **Create a Plan**: Outline a detailed action plan for achieving your short-term objectives. Include clear steps, necessary resources, potential challenges, and strategies for overcoming obstacles.

   _____

   _____

   _____

   _____

3. **Track and Adapt**: Establish metrics to monitor your progress toward your short-term objectives. How will you measure success? Describe how you will regularly review and adjust your plan to stay on track and respond to changing circumstances.

   _____

   _____

   _____

   _____

Progress Tracking

Tracking your progress is a vital part of your leadership journey. This "Progress Tracking" section of your journal is designed to help you monitor and evaluate how you are advancing toward your goals.

Start by establishing clear metrics and benchmarks that will allow you to measure your progress toward both short-term objectives and long-term goals. Use a mix of quantitative indicators, such as key performance indicators (KPIs), milestones achieved, and deadlines met, along with qualitative measures like feedback received and lessons learned.

Consistency and transparency are fundamental as you track your progress. Set regular checkpoints and review periods to evaluate your performance against your established metrics. Identify areas of strength, and pinpoint opportunities for improvement. Utilize tools and techniques such as progress dashboards, journal entries, and performance reviews to document your journey and monitor your growth over time.

Measure, adjust, advance.

When documenting your progress, aim for a balanced and realistic perspective that celebrates successes while also acknowledging setbacks and challenges. Embrace a growth mindset as you reflect on both achievements and areas for improvement. Remember, every step forward, no matter how small, contributes to your overall advancement toward your goals.

By approaching the "Progress Tracking" prompts with diligence, accountability, and a commitment to continuous improvement, you can navigate your leadership journey with clarity, resilience, and purpose, ultimately realizing your vision of success.

Progress Tracking–Journal Prompts

1. **Establishing Metrics:** Identify the key metrics and benchmarks you will use to measure your progress toward your goals. How will you know you are on track? Describe both quantitative and qualitative indicators that will help you assess your performance.

_____

_____

_____

_____

2. **Regular Checkpoints:** Outline a plan for regular progress reviews. How often will you evaluate your progress, and what methods will you use to document and analyze your performance? Consider tools like dashboards, journal entries, and performance reviews.

_____

_____

_____

_____

3. **Reflect and Adjust:** Reflect on your progress so far, celebrating your successes and acknowledging any setbacks. What have you learned from your achievements and challenges? Describe how you will use these insights to adjust your approach and continue moving toward your goals.

_____

_____

_____

_____

Additional Notes Pages

Additional Notes Pages

"We need to do a better job of putting ourselves higher on our own 'to do' list."

MICHELLE OBAMA

UNIT 8

Holistic Leadership: Embracing Wellness and Balance

This unit highlights the importance of self-care in effective leadership. Balancing the demands of leadership with personal wellness is essential. Explore strategies like stress management, work-life balance, fitness goals, and mindfulness practices. Prioritizing your well-being not only boosts your resilience but also sets an example for your team. By fostering a holistic approach to wellness, you build a foundation for sustainable success and inspire others to do the same.

This unit includes three sections of prompts:

- **Stress Management Techniques**
- **Work-Life Balance Strategies**
- **Health and Fitness Goals**

Stress Management Techniques

As you embark on your journey to become a more effective leader, it's necessary to understand the concept of stress and its impact on both your personal and professional life. Take some time to reflect on what stress means to you, and consider the various sources that can contribute to it. By identifying these sources, you can better understand how stress affects your performance and overall well-being.

Additionally, it's essential to be aware of your stress levels. Pay attention to how you're feeling, and recognize the signs that you may be getting overwhelmed. Once you notice these indicators, take proactive steps to manage your stress—whether it's taking a short break, delegating tasks, or reaching out for support.

Don't underestimate the importance of self-awareness and self-care. Taking care of yourself not only benefits you but also enhances your relationships and effectiveness as a leader. Make it a habit to regularly check in with yourself about your stress levels and integrate these stress management techniques into your daily life.

Prioritize calm and clarity.

By fostering a culture of self-care and openness about stress management among your team, you can lead by example and create an environment that prioritizes well-being. Remember, effective leadership starts with taking care of yourself!

Stress Management Techniques—Journal Prompts

1. **Techniques:** List some stress management techniques that can be used by leaders. Reflect on which ones you find the most effective and why.

   _____

   _____

   _____

   _____

2. **Looking Inward:** Consider a stressful situation you've recently been in, either personally or professionally. Why was self-awareness and self-care important in managing your stress levels?

   _____

   _____

   _____

   _____

3. **Stress and Balance:** Discuss the importance of self-care in stress management for leaders. What are some self-care strategies you have used or seen successful leaders use to manage stress and achieve balance in their personal and professional lives?

   _____

   _____

   _____

   _____

Work-Life Balance Strategies

It is important to begin this section by defining what work-life balance means to you. Reflect on your personal experiences with work-life balance and how it has impacted your leadership journey. Understanding your own experiences is vital in fostering balance within your team.

Achieving work-life balance brings numerous benefits, including increased productivity, reduced stress, and improved overall well-being. Consider how these outcomes can enhance your effectiveness as a leader.

To promote this balance, think about strategies you can adopt or share with others. Prioritize tasks, delegate responsibilities, and set clear boundaries to protect your personal time. Additionally, champion self-care activities—like exercise, meditation, and quality time with loved ones—as essential components of a healthy work-life balance.

Set boundaries; find harmony.

Implement practical tips to help your team succeed. Set realistic expectations and maintain open communication about workloads. By leading by example and creating a culture that values work-life balance, you can inspire others to achieve their own equilibrium.

Work-Life Balance Strategies–Journal Prompts

1. **Maintain Balance:** Provide three strategies you use to maintain a work-life balance.

   _____

   _____

   _____

   _____

   _____

   _____

2. **Get Back Control:** Describe what happens if you are out of balance and things are chaotic. What do you do to get control back?

   _____

   _____

   _____

   _____

   _____

   _____

3. **Define Balance:** Provide a description of work-life balance and its benefits as a leader.

   _____

   _____

   _____

   _____

   _____

   _____

Health and Fitness Goals

When writing about health and fitness goals within this unit, start by defining what wellness and balance mean to you personally. Reflect on your experiences with health and fitness and how they have shaped your leadership journey.

Setting health goals is essential for leaders. A healthy lifestyle boosts your energy, focus, and overall effectiveness. Consider the positive impact it can have on your leadership abilities.

There are some actionable steps you can take to incorporate health and fitness goals into your routine. Regular exercise, mindful nutrition, and self-care practices are essential. Prioritize these activities daily to enhance your well-being.

Balancing work demands with personal wellness is vital. Implement practical strategies like effective time management and setting boundaries to ensure you make self-care a priority.

Finally, remember to lead by example. Your commitment to health and wellness can foster a culture that encourages others in your organization to prioritize their well-being. By inspiring those around you, you create an environment where everyone can thrive.

Health and Fitness Goals–Journal Prompts

1. **Enhance Abilities:** Share your thoughts on how making time for your own health and fitness affects your abilities as a leader.

   _____

   _____

   _____

   _____

   _____

2. **Prioritizing Needs:** Reflect on a time when you struggled to balance your health goals with your leadership responsibilities. What strategies did you use to prioritize your health without sacrificing your effectiveness as a leader?

   _____

   _____

   _____

   _____

   _____

3. **Connection:** Describe the connection between health and leadership.

   _____

   _____

   _____

   _____

   _____

Additional Notes Pages

Additional Notes Pages

_____

_____

_____

_____

_____

_____

_____

_____

_____

_____

_____

_____

_____

_____

_____

_____

_____

_____

_____

_____

_____

_____

_____

_____

_____

Create Your Legacy

Leadership is not just about what you accomplish during your tenure—it's about the lasting impact you leave behind. A true leader's legacy is measured by the lives they touch, the values they instill, and the foundation they build for the future. This final chapter, "Create Your Legacy," guides you in intentionally shaping the mark you leave on your organization, your team, and the world.

"Gratitude is the healthiest of all human emotions. The more you express gratitude for what you have, the more likely you will have even more to express gratitude for."

ZIG ZIGLAR

The Heart of Leadership: Cultivating Gratitude and Recognition

This unit highlights the importance of acknowledging and honoring the contributions of others. Central to effective leadership is the ability to express gratitude authentically, recognize efforts and achievements, and create a culture where appreciation thrives.

By exploring heartfelt gestures, sincere acknowledgments, and an attitude of gratitude, this unit reveals the power of recognition in building lasting legacies. Creating an environment where every voice is heard, every effort is valued, and every contribution is celebrated helps leaders inspire, unite, and empower their teams, leaving a legacy that extends far beyond their time.

This unit includes three sections of prompts:

- **Expressing Gratitude**
- **Recognizing the Contributions of Others**
- **Cultivating a Culture of Appreciation**

Expressing Gratitude

Expressing gratitude is a powerful practice of leadership. Understanding what it means to be truly grateful and recognizing its impact is essential. Gratitude goes beyond a simple thank you; it's about acknowledging effort and achievement, which can boost motivation, improve morale, and create a positive work environment.

Gratitude can be shown in many ways—from a heartfelt conversation or handwritten note to a public acknowledgment. Each act of appreciation should be chosen to best resonate with the recipient. As a leader, these genuine gestures strengthen trust and deepen connections with your team.

Lead with "thank you."

Leaders should incorporate thankfulness into their daily interactions, taking every opportunity to recognize the dedication and achievements of those around them. Be specific in your praise, and let sincerity be the foundation of every gesture of gratitude.

Expressing Gratitude–Journal Prompts

1. **Attitude**: Describe how expressing gratitude contributes to enhanced morale, productivity, and unity within a team.

   _____

   _____

   _____

   _____

   _____

2. **Ways to Appreciate:** List the many ways leaders can show genuine appreciation to their team members.

   _____

   _____

   _____

   _____

   _____

3. **Adapting Appreciation:** Reflect on the evolution of gratitude in your leadership approach and the insights gained from this practice.

   _____

   _____

   _____

   _____

   _____

Recognizing Contributions of Others

Recognizing the contributions of others is central to effective leadership. It's important to understand the significance of acknowledgment and its essential role in motivating teams and fostering a positive workplace culture. Recognition is more than just saying "thank you"; it's about affirming the value and impact of someone's work, which boosts engagement and morale.

Think about the powerful effects of recognizing your team members' efforts. Reflect on your past experiences—how has your acknowledgment improved their performance and strengthened team dynamics? Describe the actions you've celebrated and how you expressed your appreciation, considering both immediate and long-term impacts.

The best strategy is to personalize recognition. The aim is to honor each person's unique contributions in a way that is meaningful to them. As a leader, continually seek opportunities to celebrate your team, ensuring your gestures of appreciation align with their individual preferences and aspirations.

Celebrate impacts of others' voices.

Recognizing Contributions of Others—Journal Prompts

1. **Strengthen Team Dynamics:** Recall a moment when a leader's acknowledgment notably elevated a team's motivation, inspired innovation, and bolstered collective success.

   _____

   _____

   _____

   _____

   _____

2. **Positive Culture:** Discuss the ripple effect of recognizing individual contributions on both team morale and the cultivation of a positive workplace culture.

   _____

   _____

   _____

   _____

   _____

3. **Personalized Recognition:** Reflect on a personal experience of feeling undervalued in a team setting. What recognition approach would have made you feel truly acknowledged and esteemed?

   _____

   _____

   _____

   _____

   _____

Cultivating a Culture of Appreciation

Appreciation is like the harmony that brings an organization together. This section invites you to explore what genuine appreciation means in leadership. How does recognizing and valuing others influence a team and shape its spirit?

Use real-life examples to reflect on the benefits of a workplace where appreciation is common, highlighting how it boosts individual satisfaction and team unity. Consider how leading with a positive tone sets the stage for an environment where appreciation is natural. Think about practical strategies like peer recognition programs, integrating gratitude into daily interactions, and celebrating contributions during evaluations in order to promote this culture.

Look at different ways to show appreciation, from simple spoken thanks to formal awards, and understand when and how to use each method effectively.

Most importantly, authentic recognition builds trust and connection. Without it, even the most elaborate gestures can feel empty. Embody appreciation by making it a core part of your leadership style. Watch how this transforms individuals and team dynamics.

Cultivating a Culture of Appreciation–Journal Prompts

1. **Daily Habits:** Detail strategies that seamlessly integrate gratitude and recognition into the daily workings of team interactions.

   _____

   _____

   _____

   _____

   _____

2. **Shifting Culture:** Narrate the positive shift within a team when each member genuinely feels valued and recognized for their individual contributions.

   _____

   _____

   _____

   _____

   _____

3. **Appreciation and Trust:** Discuss the role of authenticity in expressions of appreciation and its influence on fostering trust within your team.

   _____

   _____

   _____

   _____

   _____

Additional Notes Pages

_____

_____

_____

_____

_____

_____

_____

_____

_____

_____

_____

_____

_____

_____

_____

_____

_____

_____

_____

_____

_____

_____

_____

_____

_____

_____

_____

_____

Additional Notes Pages

"The delicate balance of mentoring someone is not creating them in your own image, but giving the opportunity to create themselves."

STEVEN SPIELBERG

Building Bridges: The Art of Mentorship and Expanding Your Network

This unit of your journal invites you to explore the power of relationships in fostering personal and professional growth. Mentorship, an important facet of leadership development, offers invaluable guidance, support, and wisdom from experienced mentors who have traversed similar paths. Networking, on the other hand, provides opportunities to connect with diverse individuals, exchange insights, and cultivate an atmosphere of mutual learning and collaboration. This unit serves as a dedicated space to reflect on the impact of mentorship and networking in shaping your leadership journey, fostering meaningful connections, and nurturing a legacy of mentorship and camaraderie within your life.

This unit includes three sections of prompts:

- **Mentorship Relationships**
- **Networking Contacts**
- **Key Learnings from Interactions**

Mentorship Relationships

The exploration of "Mentorship Relationships" within your journal presents an opportunity to examine the profound impact of mentorship on your leadership journey. Begin by reflecting on the mentors who have played significant roles in guiding and shaping your professional growth. Consider the qualities and attributes that make these relationships meaningful, from shared values and mutual respect to the invaluable insights and guidance they offer.

As you reflect on your mentorship experiences, investigate the specific ways in which your mentors have influenced your leadership style, decision-making processes, and career trajectory. Consider the advice, feedback, and encouragement they have provided, and reflect on how these interactions have contributed to your personal and professional development. Additionally, examine the reciprocal nature of mentorship relationships, recognizing the opportunities for learning and growth that arise from both giving and receiving mentorship.

Cultivate mutual growth.

In documenting your reflections, strive to extract actionable insights and lessons learned from your mentorship experiences. Identify the main takeaways that have had a lasting impact on your leadership approach, and consider how you can pay it forward by serving as a mentor to others. By approaching the "Mentorship Relationships" prompts with openness, gratitude, and a commitment to continuous learning, you can cultivate a legacy of mentorship that enriches not only your own leadership journey but also the lives of those you mentor.

Mentorship Relationships–Journal Prompts

1. **Impact of Mentorship:** Reflect on the impact of mentorship relationships on your personal and professional growth. Share the significant lessons you have learned from your mentor and the lasting impact of their mentorship on your leadership style, skills, and perspective.

   _____

   _____

   _____

   _____

2. **Effective Mentorship:** Explore the qualities and characteristics of effective mentorship relationships. Reflect on what makes a mentorship dynamic successful, including trust, mutual respect, open communication, and shared goals.

   _____

   _____

   _____

   _____

3. **Mentorship for Future Growth:** Reflect on how mentorship can contribute to building a strong leadership pipeline and promoting a culture of learning and growth within your organization or community.

   _____

   _____

   _____

   _____

Networking Contacts

This section of your journal is an opportunity to reflect on the diverse network of people who have enriched your professional journey. Start by listing the contacts you've made through networking, including colleagues, peers, industry leaders, and mentors. Think about the range and depth of your network, considering the different industries, fields, and perspectives represented among your contacts.

As you think about your networking experiences, consider how these connections have helped you grow professionally, collaborate with others, and learn new things. Reflect on the insights and knowledge you've gained through these interactions and how networking has expanded your opportunities and opened new doors for you. Also, consider how your networking efforts have helped create a supportive and collaborative professional community.

When documenting your reflections, try to identify common themes and patterns among your networking contacts, and note the specific ways these connections have influenced your leadership journey. Think about the opportunities for mentorship, collaboration, and knowledge-sharing that have come from your networking efforts, and explore how you can further leverage your network to support your growth and development as a leader. By approaching the "Networking Contacts" prompt with intention, curiosity, and a commitment to meaningful connections, you can build a strong network that enriches your leadership legacy and helps you succeed in your professional endeavors.

Connect with purpose.

Networking Contacts–Journal Prompts

1. **Importance of Networking:** Describe a networking experience that has been particularly impactful for you, highlighting the connections you made and the insights you gained. How did this experience shape your approach to networking moving forward? What important takeaways can you apply to future networking opportunities?

   _____

   _____

   _____

   _____

2. **Build and Maintain a Strong Network:** What specific actions do you take to cultivate and sustain your professional relationships? How do you ensure your network remains diverse and inclusive?

   _____

   _____

   _____

   _____

3. **Benefits of a Diverse Network:** How has your network contributed to your personal and professional growth? What steps can you take to further diversify and expand your network?

   _____

   _____

   _____

   _____

Key Learnings from Interactions

This important section of your journal gives you a chance to reflect on the valuable insights you've gained from your interactions with mentors, peers, and industry contacts. Start by reviewing the conversations and interactions you've had in your professional network, focusing on the main takeaways and lessons learned from these exchanges. Think about the different perspectives, experiences, and expertise shared by your contacts and how these interactions have deepened your understanding and shaped your leadership style.

As you reflect, identify common themes and patterns in your interactions. Consider the insights you've gained from discussions on leadership strategies, industry trends, and best practices, as well as the practical advice and guidance you've received from mentors and peers. Reflect on how these insights have impacted your decision-making, problem-solving, and overall effectiveness as a leader.

When documenting your reflections, aim to distill actionable insights and lessons learned from your interactions. Think about how you can apply this important information to improve your leadership skills, encourage innovation, and drive positive change in your organization. Also, explore opportunities for continued learning and growth through ongoing engagement with your professional network, recognizing the value of collaborative learning and knowledge-sharing in shaping your leadership legacy.

Seek the lesson in every encounter.

Approach the "Key Learnings from Interactions" prompts with curiosity, openness, and a commitment to continuous learning. By doing so, you can gain valuable insights that will enrich your leadership journey and help you face future challenges with confidence and resilience.

Key Learnings from Interactions—Journal Prompts

1. **Reflect on an Impactful Conversation:** Describe a specific interaction within your professional network that left a lasting impression on you. What insights or lessons did you gain from this conversation? How has it influenced your leadership approach and decision-making?

   _____

   _____

2. **Identify Common Themes:** As you review your interactions, identify recurring themes or patterns. How do these common insights shape your understanding of effective leadership? What practical strategies can you implement based on these themes?

   _____

   _____

3. **Apply Key Learnings:** Consider how you can apply the key learnings from your interactions to enhance your leadership skills and drive positive change within your organization. What specific actions will you take to integrate these insights into your leadership practice? How can you foster a culture of continuous learning and knowledge-sharing within your team?

   _____

   _____

Additional Notes Pages

_____

_____

_____

_____

_____

_____

_____

_____

_____

_____

_____

_____

_____

_____

_____

_____

_____

_____

_____

_____

_____

_____

_____

_____

_____

_____

Additional Notes Pages

"One of the things we often miss in succession planning is that it should be gradual and thoughtful with lots of sharing of information and knowledge and perspective so that it's almost a non-event when it happens."

ANNE M. MULCAHY

Future Foundations: Succession Planning and Paving the Way for New Leaders

This unit serves as a strategic pillar in ensuring the continuity and sustainability of your leadership legacy. Here, you'll embark on a journey of foresight, strategy, and intentional preparation, laying the groundwork for the seamless transition of leadership roles and responsibilities. Through thoughtful planning, talent development, and mentorship, you'll empower future leaders to step into their roles with confidence, competence, and a clear understanding of their purpose and vision. This section invites you to embrace the role of stewardship, nurturing a pipeline of leadership talent that will carry forward your legacy and propel your organization toward continued success and growth.

This unit includes three sections of prompts:

- **Identifying Potential Successors**
- **Developing a Leadership Pipeline**
- **Delegating Responsibilities**

Identifying Potential Successors

Identifying potential successors is vital for the longevity and success of your organization. This section of your journal offers a framework for recognizing, nurturing, and developing future leaders within your team. Start by evaluating the current talent in your organization, looking for individuals who show potential, capability, and commitment to step into leadership roles. Focus on qualities like strategic thinking, adaptability, and the ability to inspire and motivate others, beyond just performance and tenure.

In identifying potential successors, prioritize inclusivity and diversity. Aim to create a leadership pipeline that reflects a wide range of perspectives and experiences. Use mentorship, coaching, and leadership development programs to offer targeted support and guidance to emerging leaders. This helps them build the skills, confidence, and experience needed to excel in future leadership roles.

As you document your reflections, strive for transparency and accountability. Foster open dialogue and collaboration with potential successors as you explore their aspirations, goals, and development needs. Embrace a growth mindset as you mentor and support future leaders, recognizing that their success reflects your leadership and invests in the long-term sustainability and prosperity of your organization.

Spot commitment and capability.

By thoughtfully and inclusively working through the "Identifying Potential Successors" prompts, you can build a strong and dynamic leadership team that will foster innovation, resilience, and growth for the future.

Identifying Potential Successors—Journal Prompts

1. **Talent Assessment**: Reflect on the current landscape of talent within your organization. Identify individuals who demonstrate potential and capability for future leadership roles. Describe attributes such as strategic thinking, adaptability, and the ability to inspire others.

   _____

   _____

   _____

   _____

2. **Inclusivity and Diversity**: How can you ensure that your leadership pipeline reflects the diverse perspectives within your organization? Discuss strategies for cultivating inclusivity in your succession-planning efforts.

   _____

   _____

   _____

   _____

3. **Mentorship and Development**: Describe the mentorship, coaching, and leadership development programs you can leverage to support emerging leaders. How can these initiatives help potential successors build the skills and confidence needed for future leadership roles?

   _____

   _____

   _____

   _____

Developing a Leadership Pipeline

Creating a strong leadership pipeline is absolutely necessary for the long-term success of your organization. This section helps you identify, nurture, and grow leadership talent within your team. Start by assessing your organization's current leadership strengths and identifying gaps in skills and potential successors for leading roles. Look at factors such as skills, experience, potential, and how well individuals align with your organization's values and culture.

As you work on developing a leadership pipeline, focus on targeted development initiatives tailored to the needs and goals of potential successors. Establish leadership development programs with coaching, mentoring, and challenging assignments to provide individuals with the necessary skills and experiences for future leadership roles. Encourage a culture of continuous learning and growth, motivating potential leaders to take charge of their development and seek opportunities for improvement.

Nurture continuous growth.

Document your reflections on the progress and impact of your leadership development efforts. Highlight success stories, note challenges, and identify areas for improvement. Use your journal to record best practices, lessons learned, and insights from developing your leadership pipeline. This information will help refine and enhance your succession planning over time.

By approaching the "Developing a Leadership Pipeline" prompts with intentionality, dedication, and a commitment to talent development, you can build a strong leadership pipeline that ensures your organization's long-term success and sustainability.

Developing a Leadership Pipeline—Journal Prompts

1. **Leadership Assessment**: Reflect on your organization's current leadership bench strength. Identify any gaps in leadership capabilities and potential successors for leading roles. Consider skills, experience, potential, and alignment with organizational values.

   _____

   _____

   _____

   _____

2. **Development Initiatives**: Describe the targeted development initiatives and opportunities you can implement for potential successors. How can leadership development programs, coaching, mentoring, and stretch assignments support their growth and readiness for future roles?

   _____

   _____

   _____

   _____

3. **Monitoring Progress**: How will you track the progress and impact of your leadership development initiatives? Reflect on the success stories, challenges, and areas for improvement you've encountered in building your leadership pipeline. What best practices and lessons learned can you document and apply moving forward?

   _____

   _____

   _____

   _____

Delegating Responsibilities

Delegation is essential for developing future leaders and enhancing their capabilities. In this section, you will examine how to effectively delegate tasks and responsibilities to potential successors. Start by evaluating the strengths and skills of individuals identified as potential leaders, and consider their readiness to take on more responsibilities. Look for tasks, projects, and initiatives that match their growth goals, providing opportunities for them to develop new skills, make decisions, and work independently.

When delegating, focus on clear communication, accountability, and providing the support needed for success. Set clear expectations and goals for the tasks you delegate, and offer the guidance and resources necessary to help your successors succeed. Encourage them to take initiative and ownership of their responsibilities, contributing meaningfully to the organization's objectives.

Empower with trust.

Document your experiences with delegation, noting what worked well, any challenges faced, and the lessons learned. Provide constructive feedback and support to help your successors grow, using a coaching approach to guide them through difficulties and encourage their development.

By delegating with intention, trust, and a focus on developing talent, you can help potential successors thrive in their roles and prepare them for future leadership responsibilities within the organization.

Delegating Responsibilities—Journal Prompts

1. **Assess Readiness:** Reflect on the strengths, skills, and development areas of individuals identified as potential successors. How do you determine their readiness to take on additional responsibilities and leadership roles? What criteria do you use to evaluate their potential?

   _____

   _____

   _____

2. **Delegation Strategy:** Describe the tasks, projects, and initiatives you have delegated to potential successors. How do these align with their growth objectives, and what opportunities do they offer for skill development, autonomy, and decision-making?

   _____

   _____

   _____

3. **Support Success:** Discuss the importance of clear communication, accountability, and support in the delegation process. How do you define expectations, provide guidance, and offer resources to set potential successors up for success? What strategies do you use to encourage autonomy and initiative?

   _____

   _____

   _____

Additional Notes Pages

Additional Notes Pages

"Legacy is not
leaving something for
people. It's leaving
something in people."

PETER STROPLE

Reflections of a Legacy: Contemplating Your Leadership Journey

In leadership, the experiences, decisions, and relationships you build contribute to your legacy. This unit encourages you to take a moment to reflect on your journey—to think about the impact you've made so far and the path you want to take moving forward. Explore what defines your leadership legacy by looking at the values that guide you, the vision that inspires you, and the milestones that highlight your achievements.

As you reflect on your past, present, and future, consider how each step contributes to the legacy you wish to create. This introspective journey will help you gain insights into your leadership style, understand your core values, and envision the lasting impact you aim to leave behind. Embrace this opportunity to connect with your experiences, draw lessons from them, and chart a course for continued growth and meaningful contribution.

This unit includes three sections of prompts:

- **Value Assessment**
- **Legacy Reflection Statement**
- **Vision for the Future**

Values Assessment

This section offers a chance to think about the core principles that guide your leadership. Begin by pinpointing the values that matter most to you—those essential beliefs that steer your actions and interactions. Reflect on the experiences, both personal and professional, that have shaped these values and how they influence your everyday decisions.

Take a moment to evaluate how these values align with your leadership aspirations and the legacy you want to build. Think about how consistently you uphold these values in your leadership roles and their impact on your decision-making and relationships. Consider times when your values were put to the test and how you managed to stay true to them.

Document your reflections and think about how you can weave these values more tightly into your leadership practices. Identify specific steps to model these values, encourage your team to adopt them, and create a lasting positive impact within your organization. Use this exercise to ensure your leadership legacy stands on a solid, values-based foundation.

Align actions with core beliefs.

Approach the "Values Assessment" prompts with sincerity and a clear purpose, gaining valuable insights into your leadership journey and reinforcing your commitment to lead with integrity and purpose.

Value Assessment–Journal Prompts

1. **Core Values:** Reflect on the core values that have been central to your leadership philosophy and the legacy you aspire to leave behind. How have these values influenced your decisions, actions, and relationships throughout your leadership journey?

   _____

   _____

   _____

   _____

   _____

2. **Alignment of Values:** Explore the alignment between your personal values and the values of the organizations or communities you've led. How have you fostered a culture that reflects these shared values?

   _____

   _____

   _____

   _____

   _____

3. **Values and Legacy:** What strategies have you employed to ensure values are upheld and passed down as part of your legacy?

   _____

   _____

   _____

   _____

   _____

Legacy Statement Development

Creating a personal legacy statement involves deep reflection and self-examination. Start by thinking about the core values, beliefs, and principles that have guided your leadership journey. Reflect on significant milestones, challenges you've overcome, and pivotal moments that have shaped your understanding of leadership and your future goals.

Next, turn these reflections into a clear and concise statement that captures the essence of your leadership legacy. Your legacy statement should highlight not only your achievements but also the principles and values that define your leadership style. It should inspire and connect with others, showing the lasting impact you aim to have on your organization, community, or field.

As you develop your legacy statement, aim for clarity, authenticity, and resonance. Seek feedback from trusted mentors, colleagues, or peers to ensure it accurately reflects your values and aspirations. Remember, your legacy statement is not fixed; it should evolve as you grow and continue to make an impact. Approach this process with an open mind and heart, guided by your vision for the future and your commitment to leaving a meaningful legacy.

Define your enduring impact.

Sample Legacy Statement 1: *"I aspire to lead with integrity, empathy, and a commitment to empowering others. My legacy is one of fostering inclusive environments where diverse voices are heard, valued, and celebrated. Through my leadership, I aim to build a culture of collaboration and innovation, inspiring individuals and teams to exceed their potential. I hope to leave behind not only a record of meaningful achievements but also a lasting ripple effect of growth, kindness, and positive transformation within the communities and organizations I serve."*

Sample Legacy Statement 2:

"My leadership legacy is rooted in resilience, purpose, and service. I strive to create systems and opportunities that outlast me, enabling individuals and organizations to thrive long after my role is complete. I am committed to leading by example, embracing challenges as opportunities for growth and inspiring others to take bold action in pursuit of meaningful change. My ultimate goal is to leave a legacy of impact, driven by the belief that leadership is about building bridges, breaking barriers, and empowering others to do the same."

Legacy Statement Development–Journal Prompts

1. **Pivotal Experiences:** Reflect on pivotal moments or experiences that shaped your understanding of leadership and contributed to your legacy. How did these moments influence your leadership style and approach to creating a lasting impact?

   _____

   _____

   _____

   _____

   _____

2. **Evolution of Values:** Consider the values and principles that have guided your leadership journey. How have these core beliefs evolved over time, and how have they been instrumental in developing the legacy you wish to leave behind?

   _____

   _____

   _____

   _____

   _____

3. **Legacy Statement:** Draft your legacy statement here.

   _____

   _____

   _____

   _____

   _____

Vision for the Future

To explore your vision for the future, start by imagining the future of your organization, community, or field. Think about the challenges and opportunities ahead and how you can grow and make an impact. Let your imagination run free, and dream big about what you want to achieve.

Next, clearly define your vision, setting specific goals and outcomes you aim to reach. Consider how your leadership can help make this vision a reality, using your strengths and resources to drive positive change. Think about everyone involved and how you can bring different perspectives together to support your vision.

Imagine bold possibilities.

After reflecting on your vision, create a strategic plan with actionable steps and milestones to bring your ideas to life. Set priorities and success metrics, staying flexible to adjust to any challenges or opportunities that come your way. Embrace this visioning process as a continuous journey of innovation and collaboration, with a strong commitment to leaving a lasting legacy of positive change.

Vision for the Future–Journal Prompts

1. **Future Vision:** How do you envision the values, principles, and initiatives you have instilled during your leadership tenure shaping the trajectory of your organization or community in the years to come, and what steps can be taken to ensure their continuity and growth?

   _____

   _____

   _____

   _____

   _____

2. **Inspire Others:** How do you plan to inspire and empower emerging leaders to carry forward your vision, values, and goals?

   _____

   _____

   _____

   _____

   _____

3. **Culture of Leadership:** What strategies can be implemented to cultivate a culture of leadership excellence and sustainable impact long after your tenure?

   _____

   _____

   _____

   _____

   _____

Additional Notes Pages

Additional Notes Pages

Additional Notes Pages

CLOSING THOUGHTS: WRAPPING UP YOUR LEADERSHIP LEGACY JOURNEY

Congratulations! You've made it to the end of *Crafting Your Leadership Legacy: A Guided Journal*! We hope it has provided you with a valuable tool to cultivate intentionality and reflection in your leadership practice.

As you reflect on your journey through this journal, take a moment to consider how far you've come. You started out with a blank page and a desire to grow as a leader, and now you've got a tangible record of your progress and evolution.

Remember that growth and development as a leader is not a one-and-done process. It's an ongoing journey that requires intentional effort and reflection. Therefore, we encourage you to keep using this journal or find other tools that work for you to continue your leadership journey.

Always keep in mind that leadership is not about a title or position, nor is it a privilege that comes from being the boss. True leadership is about making positive impacts and inspiring those around you. You have the power to make a difference in the lives of those you lead—use it well.

Next Steps

This is not the end but the beginning of your journey. Use the thoughts and reflections in this journal to fine-tune your leadership skills and self-reflect on the areas you might want to expand and grow in your competencies.

To continue your leadership journey, here are some ideas you can explore to dive deeper into these concepts:

- Continue to build your network.

- Join a professional association.

- Build a vision board.

- Continue journaling, using the concepts in this book as a guide.

Thank you for trusting us to help guide your leadership journey. We hope that your use of this journal has empowered you to cultivate a more intentional and impactful approach to leadership, ensuring that your legacy reflects your values and leaves a lasting positive impact on those you lead. Onward to leadership greatness!

ACKNOWLEDGMENTS

Creating the *Crafting Your Leadership Legacy: A Guided Journal* has been an inspiring and rewarding journey—one that would not have been possible without the contributions of many remarkable individuals and communities.

To the incredible team at Lead-ology Consulting, thank you for your unwavering commitment to leadership development and your passion for helping others build their legacies. Your insights, expertise, and creativity are woven into every page of this journal.

To the countless nonprofit leaders and changemakers we've had the privilege to work with, your stories, challenges, and triumphs have deeply influenced this journal. You are a testament to the power of intentional leadership, and we are honored to support your journeys.

To our families and friends, thank you for your encouragement, patience, and belief in the importance of this work. Your support made this project possible.

Finally, to you, the leader holding this journal, thank you for taking the time to reflect on your journey and commit to building a meaningful legacy. You inspire us with your dedication to growth and the impact you strive to make in the world.

With gratitude,

Heather and Barbara

Nonprofit Leadership Experts

HEATHER GILLETTE   BARBARA MARTIN

As award-winning leaders and nonprofit leadership development consultants, we've worked for decades in PTA and nonprofit leadership.

We know what it's like to feel overwhelmed with a volunteer leader's many tasks and requirements.

After repeatedly witnessing frustrated nonprofit leaders struggle with the same problems, we noticed a common thread. These leaders wanted desperately to lead well and make an impact in the mission of their nonprofit but kept getting swallowed up in the busywork and daily grind.

That's when we started our leadership development company, presenting courses at the local, state, and national levels to help thousands of leaders just like you. To ensure we could continue to offer tools to help the nonprofit industry grow and thrive, we opened up our coaching and training business, Lead-ology. Working together as partners, we began coaching nonprofit leaders one-on-one, helping them transform into confident and intentional leaders making an impact in their organization and the world.

Because the need is so great, we've barely tapped the surface and want to do everything we can to help as many nonprofit leaders out there as possible.

Ready to take your leadership legacy to the next level?

Visit our website, lead-ology.com,
via the QR code to access exclusive tools,
resources, and merchandise designed to
support your growth as a leader.

You can sign up for our newsletters and
monthly tips to stay inspired!

www.ingramcontent.com/pod-product-compliance
Lightning Source LLC
Chambersburg PA
CBHW082226140626
46556CB00020B/3348